This Journal Belongs
To:

Made in the USA
Monee, IL
01 May 2022

95712061R00057